Communication

Acquire The Knowledge And Techniques For Fostering Effective Communication In Various Social Settings With An Insightful Exploration Of Communication Skills And A Comprehensive Manual On The Art Of Effective Interpersonal Communication

Rick Harper

TABLE OF CONTENT

Communication's Vitality 1

Overcoming Shyness 14

The Significance Of Having Empathetic Feelings In The Realm Of Health And Social Care 32

Conquer The Art Of Small Talk 52

The Importance Of Being Able To Communicate Effectively 64

The Crucial Roles That Listening And Actively Participating In Conversation Play At Work 68

Tell Some Of Your Own Personal Anecdotes ... 72

At The Office, Body Language 100

Both Confidence And Communication Are Essential For Success. 121

Why Do We Waste Our Time With Inane Chitchat? 128

Communication's Vitality

Effective communication is a paramount aspect of human existence, as it represents the fundamental skill employed by all individuals on a daily basis. We engage in spoken, non-verbal, visual, and written forms of communication. Being an effective communicator entails ensuring mutual understanding and demonstrating empathy towards others. When effective communication is established, the occurrence of assumptions is reduced, conflicts are minimized, and achieving harmonious relationships with others is facilitated. Given that communication is a reciprocal process, it encompasses both the transmission and reception of messages. Consequently, the enhancement of these aptitudes encompasses not only verbal expression but also attentive listening.

If you currently lack proficiency in communication, there is no need for concern. Acquiring proficiency in effective communication is often more attainable than commonly perceived. As you engage in the diligent application of the techniques detailed within this book, you shall progressively encounter favorable outcomes spanning various facets of your existence. Every chapter presents a systematic approach towards enhancing areas in which one may presently encounter difficulties or seeks personal refinement. In addition, enhancing one's communication skills is always advantageous, as the implementation of these exercises yields only positive outcomes. Broadening your communication repertoire possesses the potential to propel you towards unprecedented realms of success that surpass your wildest expectations. Once you begin witnessing the tangible advancements derived from the skills acquired through this book, your sole remorse shall reside in the fact that you did not commence this endeavor at an earlier point in time.

While it is commonly regarded as a soft skill, I hold a divergent view and strongly refute this perception. Effective communication is a proficiency that sets apart those who are flourishing from those who are facing challenges in their lives. They possess the ability to convey their desires to both external individuals and within their own thoughts. Maintaining a optimistic mindset through self-dialogue is essential for achieving success. Engaging in communication with individuals, in order to effectively convey your desires, serves as an initial step towards transforming your aspiration into tangible existence. Want a promotion? Inform your supervisor accordingly and subsequently execute their instructions in order to accomplish the aforementioned. Would you be interested in accompanying the lovely colleague on a social outing? Inform her of your admiration for her and inquire if she would like to join you for a coffee. Share your aspirations with the global community, and pave your path towards the attainment of your desires.

Envision the prospect of addressing an assembly, where your words transcend the understanding of not merely a single individual, but resonate coherently with the entirety of the audience. The capacity for one's voice to be attentively heard not only fosters a sense of respect, but also instills individuals with the assurance to continue expressing themselves. Now, envision the possibility of exhibiting such behavior in every interaction, reciprocating the gesture of deference to fellow individuals. Individuals desire to have their voices acknowledged, seek attentive ears, and derive satisfaction from the act of narrating their personal experiences. Provide them with the opportunity, and they will willingly reciprocate the favor to you.

Work

The workplace can evoke a sense of apprehension, particularly when your talents and contributions go unnoticed and unheard, despite your outstanding abilities. The ability to articulate your aspirations for advancement could potentially determine whether you receive the promotion, as opposed to a co-worker who may have been eligible by virtue of their longevity at the company. Based on my own firsthand observations, I have consistently witnessed this phenomenon. Individuals express dissatisfaction regarding their lack of promotional opportunities, and rather than seeking proactive solutions, they often resort to further grievances. They refrain from notifying their superiors of their aspirations for career advancement. They refrain from engaging in networking activities, they exhibit a lack of diligence in their work, and more importantly, they fail to effectively convey their aspirations for promotion to anyone. These individuals may duly communicate their aspirations to their colleagues, yet the latter possess no authority to facilitate their advancement.

Occasionally, an employment circumstance may be more adverse, such as when a supervisor harbors unfavorable sentiments towards an individual or when integrating with colleagues presents challenges. Certainly, do not abandon your aspirations due to an unfavorable working environment. Acquire proficiency in effectively addressing such challenges, for once you possess this skill, no obstacles will be insurmountable. Even if that entails employing these skills to transition to a new professional setting.

By applying the skills elucidated in this tome, you can anticipate enhanced workplace comprehension and markedly improved performance during interviews. Participating in an interview can induce a considerable amount of stress. Securing employment can be contingent upon the choice of an appropriate or inappropriate expression. Upon applying the acquired expertise, one can anticipate a heightened level of accomplishment during job interviews. One will possess the ability to establish connections expeditiously, communicate with deliberation, maintain command, concentrate attentively, deliver succinct responses, and pose apt inquiries.

Presently, it should be noted that this book does not primarily cater to individuals involved in sales; however, the ability to effectively communicate in the realm of sales is unquestionably the most essential aptitude to possess. In the sales profession, the fundamental responsibility lies in the ability to engage in effective communication. It is imperative to not only exercise attentiveness but also exhibit a keen observation of body language and timely articulation of appropriate thoughts. Enhancing your proficiency in this specific field will elevate your sales to unprecedented levels. Regardless of your professional domain, the knowledge acquired here will enhance your persuasiveness across various facets of your life.

Marriage and Relationships

Regarding the institution of marriage and interpersonal connections, there exists a crucial factor that holds utmost significance in determining the prospering of such alliances, namely effective and consistent communication. A pair who possesses the ability to comprehend, value, and effectively exchange thoughts should be capable of surmounting any obstacle. Countless divorces could be averted annually if couples were to engage in meaningful dialogue to resolve their marital issues. While this book may not possess the ability to completely quell conflicts, its contents hold the potential to enable the reader to effectively and soundly navigate through them.

The primary sources of conflict between my spouse and myself have arisen from our failure to engage in effective communication. Occasionally, it is necessary to allocate sufficient time to contemplate and analyze our true emotional state. However, on each occasion an obstacle arose, we were able to successfully overcome it through effective communication. We hold mutual love and esteem towards each other, allowing for a period of reflection in order to collaboratively resolve any issues that may arise.

Many relationships are prone to failure when either or both individuals exhibit a lack of attentive listening. As an illustrative instance, when one partner communicates a message, it fails to be received or comprehended. As this phenomenon occurs, the gradual dissolution of their connection ensues, ultimately resulting in complete cessation of communication between spouses. Further exploration of this topic will be undertaken subsequently, particularly in

which delves into the aspect of Conflict Resolution.

Social Situations

Can this book enhance your ease and confidence during social gatherings such as parties? Certainly, the primary objective of this written material is to enhance the reader's proficiency in effectively communicating across various domains of their life. Have you ever attended a social gathering where you observed an individual with the ability to engage in effortless conversations with everyone? By chance, they inadvertently collide with someone, and within a brief interval, they establish a newfound bond of camaraderie, becoming fast companions. I refer to them as individuals who are highly sociable and outgoing. I currently possess this status, although it was not the case during my earlier years. Presently, my spouse seldom permits me to independently engage in the task of grocery shopping as I have a tendency to engage in amiable conversations with fellow shoppers in the store.

It is possible to conclude that those individuals have inherently possessed the desired quality or attribute. That is not the case at all, anyone can learn to be more social. A substantial portion of this literary work is centered around the initiation and continuation of dialogue. As mentioned previously, individuals possess a strong inclination to share their personal narratives. Upon absorbing the contents of this book, you will acquire the means to provide them with this opportunity.

The primary objective of this book is not centered around increasing one's number of dates, however, the acquisition of the skills imparted within can consequently facilitate the achievement of such a goal. Initiating a dialogue or navigating through an uncomfortable initial encounter can pose a challenge for individuals regardless of their circumstances. If you presently encounter difficulty engaging in conversation during social outings or initiating contact with individuals.

Chapter 10: Initiating a Discourse will prove to be tremendously beneficial in those domains.

Expectations

What benefits can the reader anticipate obtaining from perusing this book? You can anticipate being competent in effective communication across diverse situations. Whether that entails facilitating the overcoming of a phobia, enhancing narrative prowess, or even mediating conflict resolution. There is a plethora of offerings available that cater to individuals of diverse interests and proficiency levels in the realm of communication.

The following section caters to individuals who experience apprehension in conversing with others and exhibit pronounced shyness. If this does not pertain to your circumstances, you are welcome to proceed to Chapter 3: Eye Contact. Naturally, if you are an individual seeking to peruse the contents of this book in its entirety or aiming to explore ways in which you can be of assistance to a reticent acquaintance, I highly recommend acquiring it.

Overcoming Shyness

What is shyness? It is a fear. An apprehension that hinders individuals from engaging socially, forging connections with exceptional individuals, encountering their soulmate, and a fear that thwarts individuals from realizing their aspirations in life. The sensation of timidity can be overpowering. Similar to an unforeseen impediment impeding your progress. During my early years as a firefighter, my reservoir of self-assurance seemed boundless. After engaging in interactions with several women that yielded unfavorable treatment, I gradually began to experience the emergence of apprehension.

As time elapsed, the intensity of that fear increased significantly. Every instance of rejection or mistreatment further validated my expectations and compounded my apprehensions. It reached a juncture where I developed an aversion to engaging with women. I was deeply apprehensive about facing rejection, receiving poor treatment, and potentially embarrassing myself through any inadvertent missteps, to the extent that fear completely immobilized my progress. It reached a juncture where the mere contemplation of initiating contact with an unfamiliar individual evoked feelings of anxiety within me.

What I consistently experienced was a detrimental feedback loop. A cyclical pattern characterized by an extended duration for resolution. Apprehension is acquired and generated through our own volition; it is an acquired reaction. Have you had the occasion to witness a young child in a public setting? Zero worry. While dining at a restaurant, my young son possesses the tendency to approach each table with greetings and cheerful expressions directed towards the patrons. It is worth noting that, at his age of three as of this writing, he occasionally gazes for an extended period of time. However, I kindly request your understanding and consideration towards his actions.

Naturally, there exists a rational basis for certain apprehension. The apprehension that prevents us from venturing into dimly lit passageways during nighttime serves as a commendable demonstration of indispensable fear. Essentially, any apprehension that enhances one's likelihood of survival is advantageous. Individuals have the capacity to employ fear as a proactive catalyst, a source of motivation, or an impediment to their progress. Being introverted does not pose a rational concern as establishing social connections does not compromise one's overall well-being. Indeed, encountering a life partner may potentially culminate in the miraculous act of procreation, an inherently splendid occurrence.

How Fear is Developed

Anxiety emerges surreptitiously, unbeknownst to our conscious awareness. Our subconscious mind is primarily responsible for the execution of the fear-pacifying process, thus ensuring that the corresponding reaction occurs entirely on autopilot. The generation of such fear arises from a specific type of stimulus. Allow me to illustrate my experience of developing shyness during my formative years. Prior to that moment, I had a complete absence of apprehension when it came to interacting with individuals.

The ongoing reaction to experiencing rejections from women during my initial attempts began to erode my spirit. Initially, I was able to persevere and continue with my endeavors. As the passage of time ensued, an increasing amount of apprehension began to emerge. The unfavorable reactions I was receiving were causing me to distance myself. In due course, the intensity of the fear reached such levels that it triggered an instinctive reaction of either confronting the threat or seeking immediate escape, leaving me completely immobilized in my current position. My cardiac rhythm intensified, I sensed a surge in my circulatory pressure, and I became immobilized, unable to articulate a single sound.

The fear of approaching people was solely developed as a result of recurrent exposure to unfavorable reactions. Despite receiving positive feedback, my mind would dismiss it, as if the favorable response had never occurred. That period constituted the most challenging phase in my existence. Furthermore, I encountered some challenges in my professional life, thereby exacerbating the overall negative circumstances simultaneously. The combination of this profound fear and the profoundly negative working conditions I have experienced has resulted in the most extreme state of depression I have ever encountered in my entire existence. I held a strong aversion towards women, colleagues, and most notably, had intense disdain towards my own being. I trust that this book can serve as a guiding light for individuals facing analogous circumstances, enabling them to transcend their difficulties and embark upon a more prosperous chapter in their lives.

Confidence

Describing the experience of confidence can be challenging due to its intangible nature, making it resistant to quantification. The essence of confidence lies in a sense of assuredness. Nowadays, one has the ability to cultivate confidence. The principal means of acquiring it is through taking action. Activity can encompass self-enhancement, physical exercise, essentially any endeavor that uplifts one from a despondent state and cultivates a more agreeable and optimistic frame of mind.

Nowadays, confidence comprises multiple facets and complexities. I was instructed by renowned NLP practitioner Kain Ramsey that confidence is derived from the development and personal enrichment that we encounter across the course of our lifetime. Although one may experience a sense of assurance, true confidence stems from different sources. These attributes encompass maturity, resoluteness, steadfastness, and fortitude. As one experiences advancements in these domains, their confidence is bolstered across all facets of their life. Enhancements can be made to each of these aspects, albeit comprehensive development of all these areas extends beyond the purview of this publication. Nevertheless, I shall delve into each facet to provide you with insight on how to enhance them.

Maturity comes with time. It evolves through the acquisition of knowledge, the passage of time, and a deepening understanding. As an individual's consciousness expands to encompass the intricacies of existence and its mechanisms, they accrue a greater depth of experiential knowledge. Engaging in personal development, enlisting in the armed forces, broadening your perspective, and stepping outside of your comfort zone are all means by which one can enhance their level of maturity. There is no definitive, prescribed method to cultivate maturity other than the passage of time and the accumulation of life experiences.

Decisiveness is the capacity to render determinations effectively regardless of the circumstances. The situation may entail limited information availability, a pressing time constraint, or even an exigent high-stress emergency. This feature also encompasses the capacity to assume complete accountability for all decisions, including those that may not yield favorable outcomes. Moreover, it is crucial to acknowledge that abstaining from making a choice constitutes a decision, albeit a decision to refrain from taking action. Gaining expertise in a particular field can contribute to informed decision-making. Ultimately, the essence of decisiveness lies in recognizing that one's decisions may not always be infallible, and embracing the notion that it is acceptable to err, as long as accountability is assumed and valuable lessons are derived from the experience.

Consistency refers to the capacity to maintain coherence and adhere to a steadfast commitment. This demonstrates a combination of maturity and resoluteness. Once a decision has been made, there is no room for self-doubt or reconsideration. Demonstrating steadfastness and embodying integrity through honoring one's commitments exemplifies unwavering consistency and exceptional moral character. Improving consistency requires steadfastly adhering to every commitment and promise made. Should you declare your intention to complete a chapter of the book within the present week, it is imperative that you fulfill this commitment. If you make a commitment to meet someone, it is expected that you honor it, regardless of your personal inclination. Maintain commitment and perseverance, regardless of your personal inclination.

The final element in this list pertains to resilience, specifically the capacity for emotional resilience. This pertains to the capacity to persist, even when faced with adversity in one's life. Exhibiting unwavering determination to overcome every challenge until attaining the desired objective. Emotional resilience can be cultivated through various means, including seeking assistance, enhancing one's internal dialogue, embracing vulnerability, and prioritizing self-care. All of these illustrate commendable instances; however, the most effective course of action for enhancing this domain on a broader scale is by prioritizing yourself. Make prioritizing your well-being a top task on all lists.

As evident from the aforementioned, these various domains seamlessly collaborate to not only instill a sense of assurance, but also cultivate a comprehensive individual capable of confidently maneuvering through any challenge. They possess the requisite level of maturity to adopt various viewpoints, exhibit prompt decision-making abilities, consistently demonstrate actions aligned with their beliefs, and exhibit resilience when overcoming emotional obstacles.

Exercise #2.1

Exercise #2.1 may be characterized as a cognitive exercise, originally conceptualized by Richard Bandler and John Grinder. This is a visualizing technique that will aid you in overcoming any trepidation you may possess. It has been intentionally crafted to alleviate phobias. However, it can provide assistance with any potential issue, irrespective of whether or not it elicits a phobic reaction. This exercise has the potential to be repeated an indefinite number of times. Should the initial attempt prove unsuccessful, it is advised to make another endeavor. Now, as a precautionary measure, should the visualizations exacerbate the situation, it is advised to cease engaging in them and instead seek professional assistance. I am strongly averse to exacerbating any apprehension. Prior to commencing this exercise, it is advisable to locate a conducive space for relaxation, such as a couch, or alternatively, recline on your bed.

Commence by inhaling deeply a few times.

Consider the object of your apprehension (e.g., the reluctance to initiate contact with another individual).

Now, endeavor to identify the initial occurrence during which you became subject to that feeling of fear.

Go there now.

Step out of that perception and examine yourself from an external standpoint. Envision yourself seated in a cinema. It is possible to observe a visual representation of yourself within the context of the situation that instills fear in you.

Examine the complete recollection, observe the memory unfold before you from this vantage point.

Please proceed to play the movie in reverse.

Please modify the hue to black and white as you revisit the recollection, envision progressively receding into complete obscurity as the progression nears its culmination.

Envision the sensation of effortlessly levitating from your seat within the theater and delving deep into the recesses of your memory, perceiving it once again from your initial vantage point.

Restore the memory to its original full-color state and examine it from this particular viewpoint.

Proceed to perform and iterate this exercise again, following steps five through ten, until the fear becomes sufficiently desensitized.

I decided to include this cognitive exercise as an introductory one, considering that certain individuals perusing this material may find themselves apprehensive to initiate even a simple salutation towards another individual. If such is your present state of affairs, it will cultivate robust psychological fortitude within you, enabling you to surmount the obstacle that fear has imposed upon your existence. Apprehension impedes our pursuit of personal aspirations, therefore, engage in this exercise to liberate yourself.

Exercise #2.2

Have you ever uttered a greeting or salutation to someone? If you possess excellent skills, then that is precisely what is required of you in order to successfully conclude exercise #2. Greet all individuals you encounter henceforth. If you are not inclined to smile and engage in eye contact initially, it is completely acceptable. I kindly request that you greet each and every individual you encounter henceforth with salutations such as hi, hello, what's up, howdy, or good morning/afternoon/night.

Engaging in this activity will foster self-assurance, particularly if you possess an extremely reserved disposition. If you do not possess shyness, engaging in this action will enhance your perceived friendliness beyond your current demeanor. At present, it cannot be expected that all individuals will reciprocate the greeting. Perhaps they are reticent, much like you once were. In that circumstance, kindly apprise them of the contents of this literary work. I am merely making a jest, kindly bear in mind that if someone does not respond, it should not be taken personally as individuals are preoccupied with their own individual pursuits. Perhaps by uttering a greeting, it is conceivable that you may rouse someone from slumber, thereby imparting an uplifting effect upon their day.

Enjoy your experience with this, and I eagerly await our reunion in Chapter 3: Eye Contact.

The Significance Of Having Empathetic Feelings In The Realm Of Health And Social Care

Empathy, or the capacity to comprehend the patient's personal experience without empathizing with them, is a crucial communication skill for a health practitioner. Empathy refers to the ability to feel the same emotions as another person. The emotional, the cognitive, and the behavioral aspects of a person's empathy make up the three components, forms, or compositions that make up empathy.

It has been established that medical practitioners that have a high level of empathy perform more effectively in terms of carrying out their tasks in triggering therapeutic progress. This is because they are more able to put themselves in the patients' shoes. The empathetic professional can relate to the needs of the patients since patients feel comfortable discussing their issues and wants with them.

Although it is impossible to exaggerate the importance of empathy, a disproportionately significant number of health professionals report that it is difficult to implement an empathic communication model into their day-to-day job.

Some of the variables that have a detrimental impact on the growth of empathy include the high number of patients that professionals are required to manage, a lack of sufficient time, the emphasis placed on therapy within the current academic culture, and the absence of instruction in empathy.

The cultivation of empathetic skills need to be the central focus of education at the undergraduate level in the fields of health and social care, as well as the primary focus of continuing education throughout a career for professionals.

According to some sources, effective communication is the ability that is most essential for a health practitioner to possess. For there to be effective communication between the therapist and the patient, the therapist must be sure that they have accurately grasped the patient's needs and noted them in order to provide tailored care.

It is essential for medical professionals to have an in-depth comprehension of their patients' thoughts, feelings, and experiences in order to correctly determine the patients' actual requirements and provide the necessary level of specialized care in response. The development of skills in empathy is required in order to accomplish this goal.

The concept of empathy is held dear by a large number of professionals working in the medical field, including nurses, doctors, psychiatrists, and social workers. Since its inception, teaching and implementation of clinical social practice have been guided by the person-centered approach, which prioritizes complete acceptance of the individual receiving medical care as well as empathy for that person.

Participants in a recent study described empathy as the ability to understand and experience the feelings, ideas, and wishes of others, as well as the capacity to comprehend the emotional and cognitive condition of the person with whom one is interacting in the capability of a health worker to comprehend the emotional and cognitive condition of the person with whom one interacts.

In conclusion, one may say that empathy is a combination of the cognitive, emotional, and practical capacities that are required in order to provide for a patient.

Empathy has been shown to play a significant part in the overall improvement of health outcomes and is one of the primary therapeutic interactions that should exist between medical professionals and the people they treat.

It is beneficial to the expansion and development of the therapeutic connection between the two parties since it makes it possible for medical professionals to recognize and comprehend the experiences, concerns, and viewpoints of the patients. It is a widely held belief that having skills in empathy might improve therapeutic outcomes when employed in the healthcare field.

The medical staff's ability to empathize with the individuals who get their care boosts their ability to collaborate in the development of a treatment plan and an individualized intervention, which in turn increases the patient's level of satisfaction with the therapeutic process. When this is done, the overall treatment is of higher quality, there are fewer errors made, and a greater number of patients receive therapy that they feel is beneficial to them. In addition, it has been demonstrated that the sympathetic relationship that develops between caregiver and patient throughout the course of care enhances the therapeutic effects since patients are more likely to adhere to the therapeutic plan of action.

Research that was carried out on a variety of patient demographics and dealt with a wide array of health problems yielded optimistic findings about the overall health of the patients. Empathy has been linked to excellent treatment outcomes for a variety of conditions, including diabetes, according to research that focused specifically on diabetic patients. In addition, patients with cancer who get compassionate nursing care exhibit lower levels of stress, despair, and animosity during their treatment. Because of this, expectant moms who have a relationship with a midwife in which they feel safe, trusted, and supported have higher levels of satisfaction and experience far less stress, unhappiness, and pain during childbirth.

Empathy and comprehension should serve as the cornerstones of the relationship that exists between a healthcare practitioner and their patient. When this happens, patients experience a sense of security and trust in the abilities of the expert who is treating them.

As a consequence of this, the gap that existed between the specialist and the patient is bridged, and both parties progress toward one another, thereby realizing the benefits of this relationship. The quality of life of the therapists is improved, and they suffer less stress and burnout on the job as a result of a connection that is founded on empathy. It has been shown that medical professionals who have higher levels of empathy experience less feelings of depression and burnout in their careers.

Empathy is given a high priority in the social care and health industries. It has been emphasized that the social worker's capacity for empathy and understanding of the users' experiences and feelings plays an important role in social care. This is because empathy is one of the most important talents that social workers can employ to develop a therapeutic connection.

Empathy, or the capacity to comprehend the patient's personal experience without empathizing with them, is a crucial communication skill for a health practitioner. Empathy refers to the ability to feel the same emotions as another person. The emotional, the cognitive, and the behavioral aspects of a person's empathy make up the three components, forms, or compositions that make up empathy.

It has been established that medical practitioners that have a high level of empathy perform more effectively in terms of carrying out their tasks in triggering therapeutic progress. This is because they are more able to put themselves in the patients' shoes. The empathetic professional can relate to the needs of the patients since patients feel comfortable discussing their issues and wants with them.

Although it is impossible to exaggerate the importance of empathy, a disproportionately significant number of health professionals report that it is difficult to implement an empathic communication model into their day-to-day job.

Some of the variables that have a detrimental impact on the growth of empathy include the high number of patients that professionals are required to manage, a lack of sufficient time, the emphasis placed on therapy within the current academic culture, and the absence of instruction in empathy.

The cultivation of empathetic skills need to be the central focus of education at the undergraduate level in the fields of health and social care, as well as the primary focus of continuing education throughout a career for professionals.

According to some sources, effective communication is the ability that is most essential for a health practitioner to possess. For there to be effective communication between the therapist and the patient, the therapist must be sure that they have accurately grasped the patient's needs and noted them in order to provide tailored care.

It is essential for medical professionals to have an in-depth comprehension of their patients' thoughts, feelings, and experiences in order to correctly determine the patients' actual requirements and provide the necessary level of specialized care in response. The development of skills in empathy is required in order to accomplish this goal.

The concept of empathy is held dear by a large number of professionals working in the medical field, including nurses, doctors, psychiatrists, and social workers. Since its inception, teaching and implementation of clinical social practice have been guided by the person-centered approach, which prioritizes complete acceptance of the individual receiving medical care as well as empathy for that person.

Participants in a recent study described empathy as the ability to understand

and experience the feelings, ideas, and wishes of others, as well as the capacity to comprehend the emotional and cognitive condition of the person with whom one is interacting in the capability of a health worker to comprehend the emotional and cognitive condition of the person with whom one interacts.

In conclusion, one may say that empathy is a combination of the cognitive, emotional, and practical capacities that are required in order to provide for a patient.

Empathy has been shown to play a significant part in the overall improvement of health outcomes and is one of the primary therapeutic interactions that should exist between medical professionals and the people they treat.

It is beneficial to the expansion and development of the therapeutic connection between the two parties since it makes it possible for medical professionals to recognize and comprehend the experiences, concerns, and viewpoints of the patients. It is a widely held belief that having skills in empathy might improve therapeutic outcomes when employed in the healthcare field.

The medical staff's ability to empathize with the individuals who get their care boosts their ability to collaborate in the development of a treatment plan and an individualized intervention, which in turn increases the patient's level of satisfaction with the therapeutic process. When this is done, the overall treatment is of higher quality, there are fewer errors made, and a greater number of patients receive therapy that they feel is beneficial to them. In addition, it has been demonstrated that the sympathetic relationship that develops between caregiver and patient throughout the course of care enhances the therapeutic effects since patients are more likely to adhere to the therapeutic plan of action.

Research that was carried out on a variety of patient demographics and dealt with a wide array of health problems yielded optimistic findings about the overall health of the patients. Empathy has been linked to excellent treatment outcomes for a variety of conditions, including diabetes, according to research that focused specifically on diabetic patients. In addition, patients with cancer who get compassionate nursing care exhibit lower levels of stress, despair, and animosity during their treatment. Because of this, expectant moms who have a relationship with a midwife in which they feel safe, trusted, and supported have higher levels of satisfaction and experience far less stress, unhappiness, and pain during childbirth.

Empathy and comprehension should serve as the cornerstones of the relationship that exists between a healthcare practitioner and their patient. When this happens, patients experience a sense of security and trust in the abilities of the expert who is treating them.

As a consequence of this, the gap that existed between the specialist and the patient is bridged, and both parties progress toward one another, thereby realizing the benefits of this relationship. The quality of life of the therapists is improved, and they suffer less stress and burnout on the job as a result of a connection that is founded on empathy. It has been shown that medical professionals who have higher levels of empathy experience less feelings of depression and burnout in their careers.

Empathy is given a high priority in the social care and health industries. It has been emphasized that the social worker's capacity for empathy and understanding of the users' experiences and feelings plays an important role in social care. This is because empathy is one of the most important talents that social workers can employ to develop a therapeutic connection.

Patients who report experiencing empathy from their caregivers report better treatment outcomes and stand a better probability of showing signs of improvement. In addition, social workers who have higher levels of empathy are better able to carry out the duties of their employment in a way that is both effective and productive in terms of meeting the obligation they have to bring about social change. This occurs as a result of the social worker's ability to comprehend and have sympathy for their healthcare clients, which in turn makes it easier for the clients to feel comfortable sharing their thoughts and concerns. Empathy makes this possible. When this is done, a foundation of trust is established, which not only facilitates therapeutic progress but also enhances the care recipient's general social functionality.

A person's capacity to carry out daily tasks (such as preparing and maintaining meals, looking for housing, taking care of oneself, and commuting) and their capacity to fulfill social roles (such as a parent, employee, or community member) in accordance with the requirements of their cultural environment are both evaluated by the social worker. Social functionality levels refer to a person's ability to carry out daily tasks (such as preparing and maintaining meals) and their capacity to commute.

Empathy is a key factor in arriving at an accurate assessment of the situation that the patient is in. It enables therapists to effectively regulate the user's emotions by making use of non-verbal signs such as behavior modeling, body language, tone of voice, and other similar cues.

Empathy, in addition to making it simpler for the user to comprehend the world around them, also improves the user's quality of life.

Conquer The Art Of Small Talk

Mastering the art of small talk is an absolute must if you aspire to develop strong conversational skills. Mastering the art of idle chatter is not only beneficial on a personal level, but it will also serve you well in your professional life if you can do it well. Have you ever been chatting to someone and found that you ran out of topics to talk about? If so, how did you handle the situation? You find yourself stuck in an uncomfortable stillness, waiting for any kind of distraction to emerge, don't you? Do you find yourself wishing for any kind of covert exit whenever you're in a position like this? Now that you've found this chapter, you may put your worries to rest since you'll soon be an expert in the art of making small chat.

What exactly is "Small Talk"?

What exactly is the meaning of "small talk"? It's the kind of talk that typically takes place between people you don't know very well. It makes it possible for the individuals to judge one another in a way that is both friendly and professional. It is a straightforward approach that can result in fruitful interactions with other people. If you do things the right way, you may build relationships with people that will last a lifetime, whether they be friends, colleagues, or business associates. The transformation of unfamiliar connections into familiar ones can be aided by engaging in small conversation. If you put it to productive use, it will be much simpler for you to get through the day and engage in conversation with new individuals. Additionally, you can utilize it to communicate your thoughts while simultaneously constructing an impressive framework for further communication.

The use of small talk as a conversational filler is highly recommended. During a conversation, it is considered rude and uncomfortable to be silent for an extended period of time. If, even after a few of minutes, it seems as though you've lost the thread of the conversation, you can get it back on track by engaging in some light banter. If it seems like the other person isn't interested in continuing the conversation, you should give them the opportunity to depart on their own terms.

Another advantage of engaging in idle chatter is that it might keep talks from petering out unexpectedly. When a conversation is cut off unexpectedly, it can give the other person the impression that they have been rejected. You can prevent something like this from taking place by engaging in idle chatter. Conversational small chat is a useful tool for shifting the focus away from a weighty subject and onto something more lighthearted. Because of this, it is much simpler to avoid any awkwardness and might make it possible for you to conclude any conversation on a positive note.

Advantages to Engaging in Chit-Chat

Even though it is referred to as small talk, when employed appropriately, it can give major benefits to those who engage in it. The following is a list of some of the benefits that coming up with small chat can bring.

Informing others in a short amount of time can be accomplished quite effectively through the use of small conversation. You are also able to assess the setting thanks to this ability. You can utilize it to learn more about the person you are attempting to have a conversation with. It enables you to leave an impression on someone that will stay a long time.

Conversation with complete strangers or even just acquaintances can be an excellent way to generate new thoughts and ideas. When you are talking to someone, you probably have one goal in mind: to make a good impression on them. This indicates that you are considering new subjects, potential solutions to problems, or other matters of a similar nature in an effort to locate some points of agreement. You are given the opportunity to think creatively as a result of this.

Small conversation was the beginning of everything, whether it was a relationship with a close friend or even with a partner. All of this started somewhere and at some point. Every friendship needs to get off to a good start. You never know who you might find up talking to, and you might form a connection with someone that will last a lifetime just from casual conversation. Therefore, you should refrain from ignoring it and instead concentrate on making the most of any opportunity you have to engage in conversation with other people.

Mastering the Art of Casual Conversation

Making casual conversation is the most effective method for enhancing your ability to interact with new people. There is no better time than the present to get started if you feel that these abilities have become a little rusty or that you need to work on honing them. It doesn't matter if you're at a cocktail party or a business meeting; making small conversation is not always as simple as it seems to be in those situations. The act of striking up a conversation with a complete stranger might, at times, be little painful or highly awkward. On the other hand, just as with anything else in life, you need to keep practicing in order to get better, and ultimately, you will become an expert at making small conversation. You are not required to strive for perfection, and this is the only thing you need to keep in mind. If you keep working on it, you will soon be able to enjoy the advantages of your hard work.

Method of IFR

This is an effective method for keeping the conversation exciting while also maintaining a sense of equilibrium. IFR is an abbreviation that stands for enquire, follow up, and relate, and it is the name given to this strategy. The use of this strategy prevents you from asking an excessive number of questions in a succession or from focusing too much attention on oneself.

When employing this strategy, the first thing you will need to do is inquire, which is posing an honest query to the target audience. The next thing that you need to do, which is the second step, is to ask a follow-up question after this. The third stage is to tell the other person something about yourself that is connected to what they have told you. This information should be relevant to what they have told you. After this, you will be able to restart the process by posing another honest inquiry into the system.

For instance, if you go to a party and you talk to someone who later reveals that they are a movie director, you may certainly ask them about the genre of films that they produce. After they have provided an answer, you have the opportunity to ask them a follow-up question about a particular interest of theirs or anything else connected to the movies they have produced. And then, all that is left for you to do is say something that is in agreement with the response that they have provided.

Method of the ARE

You can facilitate small chat using another method known as ARE, which is quite similar to the IFR technique that was discussed earlier in this paragraph. Anchor, Reveal, and Encourage are the three words that make up this acronym. The steps that need to be followed are as follows.

The first thing you need to do is come up with a "anchor." When using an anchor, you are essentially required to see a reality that is mutual or shared with other people. It might be something you are experiencing or something you are watching. Either one works. This will change depending on the environment in which the encounter takes place. For instance, if you happen to run into someone at the grocery store and see that you are both purchasing the same item, you can use this as an anchor to begin a conversation with that person.

The next step is called the "reveal." In this part of the process, you will need to say something that ties to the anchor that was discussed in the previous stage. You may make a comment about how the watermelons are on sale in the grocery store, for instance, if you observe that they are marked down. You may also consider using a different narrative or an incident that is analogous to the one being discussed in order to keep the conversation continuing.

To "encourage" the conversation is the final stage, but it is most certainly not the least important step. You can accomplish this by asking a question that is open-ended or something that is more detailed that is connected to the second stage. For instance, if you want to start a discussion with someone when you are at the grocery store, you could ask them a question about something general or specific, such as "what do you think about these melons?" Alternatively, "what do you think about this deal?"

To summarize

Let's briefly review some of the most important topics that were covered in this chapter:

To hone your ability to communicate with others, you will need to become proficient in the art of idle chatter, sometimes known as small talk.

Small talk is an important skill that can be used in every interaction. It has the following benefits: it helps keep the conversation moving smoothly, it allows you to gauge other people, and it can help convert connections from being unfamiliar to being familiar.

IFR (Inquire, Follow-up, and Relate) and ARE (Anchor, Reveal, and Encourage) are two conversational strategies that need to be mastered in order to become an expert in the art of small talk.

The Importance Of Being Able To Communicate Effectively

The degree to which we are able to communicate successfully has an effect on every facet of our lives. It has the potential to impact our relationships, the atmosphere in which we work, the level of success we achieve in our careers, and how we behave in social settings. People who are able to communicate well tend to have more happiness and have greater levels of achievement.

In recent years, there has been a greater emphasis placed on efficient communication as a result of research that has demonstrated how vitally crucial it is for our day-to-day lives. These days, a course in interpersonal communication is a required component of the fundamental studies at the majority of educational institutions. However, things weren't always like this. There are many people living in our world who have never received any kind of formal education and so have no idea how to communicate successfully in this day and age.

There is a significant number of kids that leave high school with the intention of going straight into the workforce or to a trade school, despite the fact that college is still strongly encouraged for a number of graduating students. In addition, these people are uneducated and lack the abilities necessary for interpersonal contact. There will always be people in the world who lack the ability to communicate on the most fundamental level as long as our culture does not make education about these topics a priority at the secondary level.

Because of a lack of education in interpersonal communication, multiple generations of people have grown up unable to understand how to communicate effectively in the modern world. Because of this, there has been a startling rise in the number of persons who suffer from social anxiety. If you suffer from social anxiety, one of the most effective ways to reduce that fear in any social setting is to learn how to communicate clearly and effectively with the people around you.

Know that you are not alone in your struggle to be comprehended, regardless of the motivations behind your lack of education in the field of communications. Every day, the ability to communicate clearly and concisely is a challenge for thousands of people. It is not something to be ashamed about. You have already taken the first significant step in enhancing your ability to communicate with other people simply by picking up this book.

There are a lot of books on communication skills, and many of them contain exercises that are designed to make you feel ridiculous, such as talking to yourself in front of a mirror. You will not be practicing in such a manner after reading this book. Instead, we are going to look at the four characteristics of good communication, how they can be applied to every circumstance that may arise in your life, as well as some useful techniques to improve these skills.

The Crucial Roles That Listening And Actively Participating In Conversation Play At Work

Planning, leading, organizing, and overseeing are all fundamental management responsibilities that must be fulfilled. Effective communication is essential for any manager who want to fulfill all of these responsibilities successfully. One of the primary reasons that a group of individuals with varying personalities, management styles, cultural backgrounds, and other factors may successfully work together toward the accomplishment of a common objective is because of effective communication.

It is impossible to place enough emphasis on the significance of clear and effective communication in the workplace. It is one of the crucial factors that can make or break any company, and it is essential to the accomplishment of any organization's goals and objectives. In point of fact, a lack of communication is the root cause of many issues that arise in business partnerships, and the incorrect interpretation of data frequently makes things even more complicated.

Communication in the workplace is essential for a number of reasons, including the following:

1. Contributes to the Maintenance of a Healthy Working Environment

Employee motivation is one of the most critical factors that determines the level of an organization's success. When there is clear and consistent communication between employees and management, everyone is aware of what is expected of them, which makes it more likely that employees will fulfill their responsibilities to a high standard. When these two parties have open lines of communication with one another, there is less opportunity for frustration and confusion to arise in the workplace.

2. It Assists in the Elimination of Cultural Obstacles

Diversity in the workplace has the potential to lead to many misconceptions if there is insufficient emphasis placed on effective communication. When everyone in a business setting is able to understand and put appropriate communication into practice, linguistic and cultural differences may be managed effectively.

3. Decreases the Number of Employees Who Quit and Absenteeism

Effective communication in the workplace is an excellent predictor of job happiness. This is due to the fact that individuals who understand their positions in the company and are able to communicate both upward and downstream are more likely to be content with their jobs. A healthy flow of ideas, thoughts, and concerns in the workplace is made possible through effective communication, which is shown to have a favorable impact on absenteeism and employee turnover rates.

4. Encourages Collaboration as well as Professional Relationships

When effective communication is practiced, teamwork and professional relationships are enhanced because it enables tough or negative messages to be correctly expressed without eroding trust or causing conflict. This is because good communication enables difficult or negative messages to be communicated properly.

Tell Some Of Your Own Personal Anecdotes.

A great number of live performers or presenters are able to engage with the content they are providing and still convey it effectively at face value.

It takes a completely different set of skills to be able to relate a personal experience to a stranger in the same way that you would to a close friend or member of your family, yet doing so can make all the difference. People that make it a point to tell the audience about the history of what they are presenting and explain why the information they are providing is significant to them are typically the most effective speakers and performers at engaging the audience in my experience.

When it comes to poets or singer-songwriters, telling anecdotes or stories to the audience might offer them with knowledge that adds another layer of meaning and depth to a poem or song they were already familiar with and enjoyed, but which they may not have completely appreciated before. It could also provide more of a human touch to something that they are possibly hearing for the first time, which would make it more probable for them to pay attention and take something valuable away from it, as opposed to merely turning the pages of their book or tuning their guitar strings in quiet.

If you don't stop them, a significant portion of the audience might be tempted to check their phones, engage in social media activity, or converse with one another. When I went to see a band perform live in Kentish Town, London, they skipped over the traditional "closing track" introduction and went straight into their encore song. When this song started playing, the girl sitting next to me didn't look up from the book she was reading by the light of the torch, nor did she respond in any other way.

As opposed to merely spewing forth a never-ending torrent of one-liners, stand-up comedians are typically at their most successful when they draw on longer anecdotes that are based on their own personal experiences. If a performer relies too heavily on one-liners, they run the risk of their performance coming off as forced, overly slick, or shallow. One-liners can be wonderful when used in moderation, though.

When motivational speakers share their own personal "rags to riches" experiences, they frequently have the greatest impact (and I'm not simply speaking to financial gains). On the other hand, this stands in stark contrast to those who merely spread information without actually providing a compelling cause for others to accept their word for it. The audience may be wondering, "This is great, but how do I know that this stuff works?" if there is not sufficient anecdotal proof presented.

When presenters share their own experiences, it can lend credibility to the counsel they offer and provide additional impetus for the audience to pay attention. If there is an option for audience members to raise their hands and make remarks in this manner, it can also help people feel more obliged to share some of their own personal experiences that are pertinent to the topic being discussed.

You should treat others the way you would like to be treated yourself.

Consider the following scenario: you decide to grab a cup of coffee with a close friend, member of your family, or significant other. How would you feel if they spent the entire conversation, or major chunks of it, fidgeting and staring at the ceiling or the floor, and very little of the talk looking you in the eye, smiling, and using facial expressions? How would it make you feel?

How far away?

Were you cut off?

Perhaps even less than it deserves.

When communicating with individuals or with big groups of people, the fundamental approach should be the same as when communicating with a single person.

You do not want to give the impression that you are treating the people who are in the room with you as if they are not there or as if you would rather to be somewhere else.

It is recommended that you steer clear of simply practicing the material and delivering it word for word without making any effort to engage the audience. Instead of approaching the performance as a practice that just so happens to be in front of a room full of people, you will be more present in the moment if you make an effort to talk off the cuff. If you treat the performance like a rehearsal, you will not be as present in the moment.

Those who are not accustomed to it may find it intimidating to speak on the spur of the moment, which was certainly the case for me. If you are about to do something that the compère or certain members of the audience have seen you do in the past, you may make a joke about how you are sorry to bore them by repeating some of the same material on multiple occasions and say that you are sorry for boring them.

You could comment about how slippery the stage is and how, if you had known it was going to be like that, you would have worn shoes that had more traction.

In general, observations and comments should be made while maintaining a cheerful tone.

Even if it is just momentarily when glancing up from a page or an instrument, making the effort to look people in the eye sounds like such a basic concept, and the last thing I want to do is state the obvious, but it is astonishing how few people actually do this. Even if it is just momentarily when glancing up from a page or an instrument.

Eye contact with the audience can be daunting or off-putting for some presenters, which is understandable given that it can be for people who are not used to it. However, it is something that can grow easier with experience as you become more accustomed to speaking in front of crowds. Those that make it a priority to break past this barrier, even if it has to be done in small increments, will be rewarded with the ability to start building more camaraderie with whoever is watching.

It is not required to give a full discussion or performance without using a microphone. It is possible that persons who have medical conditions that affect their voice or who have gone unplugged for extended periods of time without receiving enough vocal training should avoid doing so. Nevertheless, it has the potential to be a very successful crowd-pleaser even if it can only be done for the occasional word or sentence. It is possible for it to appear to be less artificial, and it is possible for the audience to have a more natural and genuine connection to the speaker as a result.

There isn't a huge gap between being confident in your abilities and acting arrogant about them. People with enormous egos do not receive a positive response from audiences, and you should not expect one either.

TAROT CARD OF THE EMPRESS

Is it a good sign if you get the Empress in a reading about your love life? The correct response is "yes," and the reason for this is that the Empress exemplifies love. She is a symbol of love and being nurtured. She is mature, caring, and sensitive beyond her years.

Because the Empress exudes such profound love, she inspires you to have trust in everything (regardless of how horrible it is) and that everything will be okay. Through the Empress's love, you will find the strength to cure your inner child.

The Empress Is Love, and Because She Is Love, She Is Successful The Empress is successful because love is the greatest success of all in the end.

People will gravitate toward you like a moth to a light if they feel that they can relate to you in the same way that the Empress does. People adore being in your company, and you might have noticed that they benefit more from being in your presence than you do from theirs when you're in their company. People always leave a conversation with you feeling much better about themselves and about life in general, and this is mostly due to the fact that you exude an air of optimism and positivity in everything you do. Your twin flame's higher self is in awe of your ability to heal the lives of others and of how intuitive you are growing to be. Both of these abilities have amazed your twin flame. You are the kind of person who can be counted on to be steady and reliable in a relationship.

When it comes to love, the energy you are putting off right now is one of patience, and you are not desperate about anything. You have faith in love, and you are certain that it can never be betrayed or let down. Your twin flame is really fortunate to have someone like you in their life.

The Empress represents someone who will love you so profoundly that it will make your life feel like it is abundant in every way. This person is associated with your twin flame.

17

TAROT CARD OF THE EMPEROR

The Emperor card is symbolic of a love that can both comfort and torment its recipient at the same time. The higher self of your twin flame has a lot of expectations for you, both in terms of your work life and your personal life. The Emperor's devotion comes with a great deal of responsibility because there is frequently a career-related, financially-related, or family-related concern that is tied to the connection.

The emperor has a greater breadth of experience than you have and occupies a more elevated position in society. Being in the Emperor's company automatically elevates one's social standing in the wider world. You will no longer have to think about or hope for what it would be like to live in particular circles while having abundance and prosperity because you will really experience it. If you have ever thought about or desired what life would be like in these circumstances, you will now live it. The fact that you and your twin flame are in the same physical location does not mean that you share the same universe in its whole, the Emperor; your twin flame does not let you into its innermost recesses. You can expect to find yourself a little bit on the outside of things, which is where your growth will occur. Whether you like it or not, you will become an enlightened spiritual being as well as a person of refined elegance and exquisite flavor.

Stability and safety are both represented by the Emperor. There is no one who can avoid going through the dark night of the soul. When traveling with the Emperor on the path of the twin flame, one should always be prepared for challenging spiritual lessons. There will be teachers that come into your life in the form of children, family members, twin flames, and friends who will teach you things about your heart and spirit. You will find that there are occasions when you will question whether or not you would have been happy with someone who was less successful.

The majority of people who get into relationships with Emperors have heightened levels of intuition and creativity as a means of keeping up with everything that is going on.

Why does communication even matter so much in the first place?

There are numerous modes of communication, the most common of which are verbal and nonverbal. Non-verbal communication encompasses not only body language but also non-verbal indicators like tone of voice and facial expressions in addition to spoken and written language. Verbal communication encompasses both spoken and written language. It is essential that both your verbal and nonverbal modes of communication are consistent with one another. When it comes to dealing with more personal concerns, certain modes of communication are likely to be ineffective, despite their potential efficacy in other contexts, such as academic or professional environments.

Developing and sustaining any kind of connection is impossible if communication cannot take place between the parties involved. According to the research conducted by Psychologist Robin Dunbar, "language evolved as a way of allowing larger and larger numbers of individuals to live and work together in ever-larger social groups." To put it another way, language gives us the ability to communicate with other people and to form meaningful connections.

The ability to communicate effectively is key to dispute resolution. If you are able to articulate your thoughts precisely and listen to the perspectives of others without judging them, it will be much simpler to find a solution that satisfies the needs of all parties involved. Understanding one another and avoiding misconceptions are two of the most important aspects of good communication. You will always be able to say the appropriate thing to say if you take the time to carefully create a message and consider how your audience will understand what you've expressed to them. The cultivation of trust is facilitated by communication. When you are able to communicate clearly and successfully with another person, they are more likely to regard you as trustworthy and dependable. They are going to have a much easier time opening up to you and putting their trust in you. This is of the utmost significance in romantic partnerships, when it is essential to have the sense that one can count on one's companion. Trust is another essential component of collaboration; if members of a team do not trust one another, they will not be able to collaborate effectively and produce the best possible outcomes for their efforts.

In conclusion, having strong communication skills is necessary for your own personal satisfaction. It doesn't matter if you're looking for a new job, expanding your social network, or navigating a family gathering or social function: having the capacity to communicate successfully will help you attract the kind of people that make you feel comfortable and allow you to be yourself. This is true whether you're looking for a new career, building up your social network, or navigating a family gathering or social function. People who are able to express their ideas and views in a concise manner are more likely to leave a favorable impression on the people they meet and to differentiate themselves from the throng.

What is one promise made by a public relations firm that, if it were made to you, would cause you to be suspicious of the agency that is trying to win your business?

The response is basic and easily understood. And the majority of those of us sitting on the other side of the table, known as the client side, are very familiar with this response. It is the promise of column inches in print, air-time in news channels, and news-time in general entertainment, news, or business channels — basically any aspect of the media.

Column inch and air-time promises are provided on a platter, and even stated in the RFP's by the clients inviting pitch, now that there is a swathe of public relations agencies of every color and colour in the world. Not to mention a handful of self-styled public relations gurus and their clan.

When one or more brands or organizations are assured of such strange public relations promises, merely for the sake of it, rather than on the basis of any sound foundation, then it becomes irresistible for a host of others to come up with such requests in the RFI. This results in a vicious loop, in which organizations continue to make ever more column centimeter promises without actually caring about whether or not they will be able to deliver on those promises in practice.

It is no longer effective to drive PR with column centimeters; anyone who still does it in the hope of landing a prospective client runs the danger of losing his credibility and engaging in a fruitless pursuit. In almost all of these scenarios, there is a significant chance that the sales team that comes in to give the presentation and make numerous promises will not even be seen again after the account is won. In many instances, and particularly with major global public relations megaliths, the actual team that serves the account on a day-to-day basis may be quite different from the one that came in with the first pitch. This is because of the nature of the work that is required to maintain the account.

Not only that, but what else is going on here? How do you want others to perceive you when they read the news? In print or via radio or television? Is it relevant to your ideal customers, the product you want to market, and the market that you operate in... There are a great number of unknowns regarding the PR outcome in relation to the real media coverage that you require.

It's impossible for every company to be as successful as Apple or the Indian software giant Infosys, where tons of column inches, even when they're negative, make perfect sense. Would this be acceptable for your firm and its brand?

If this is not the case, then it is unclear why you would fall into the PR pitch that offers you the column centimeter moon. Examine the particulars, along with the context, the positioning, and the time of the event. These are the elements that should be considered when deciding whether or not the coverage or visibility is relevant.

Examine how well PR measures up against the overall context of the situation. Without fail.

That will make a great deal more sense than simply painting image stripes on your 'cat brand' and attempting to imitate the tiger in any way.

How one perceives oneself and how one sees oneself

A conscious as well as an unconscious manner of perceiving oneself is what we mean when we talk about having a self-image. This is the emotional assessment that we have made regarding the value of ourselves. We develop our sense of who we are as individuals by engaging in conversations with other people and paying attention to the responses they provide to us and the labels they assign to us. Their perspective on the world determines how they will react to us, and this dynamic may hinder them from having an appropriate self-perception as a result.

Despite their best efforts, human beings cannot help but compare themselves to those around them. People have a tendency to evaluate themselves in accordance with the expectations of their family and friends. The majority of the time, society assigns us a particular role, such as being a responsible parent or having a successful career. This can have an effect on the way that we perceive ourselves.

We are always conducting an evaluation of ourselves. When we have a healthy, optimistic view of ourselves, we are more likely to accept and value ourselves, which in turn can boost our confidence. A poor opinion of ourselves might put us in a downward spiral that can lead to feelings of inadequacy or sadness. People who cultivate a self-image that is both realistic and mature won't come unglued in response to every unfavorable comment they get.

When you have a low sense of self-worth, you have a tendency to view yourself, the world, and your future with a more negative and critical outlook. It's possible that you'll have feelings of anxiety, sadness, and poor motivation. When you are faced with difficulties, you could question whether or not you have the ability to overcome them. In your head, you might berate yourself by saying things such, "You're stupid," "You'll never manage this," or "I don't amount to anything."

The core of having low self-esteem is found in the unfavorable thoughts and perspectives that you have about yourself. These are the kinds of views that only emerge when a person goes through life and gain exposure to new things; no one is born with them. How you are treated by other people, particularly while you are growing up, can have a tremendous impact on your perception of who you are.

The encouraging news is that overcoming low self-esteem is not as difficult as one might think. In order to overcome this negative view of oneself, there are two essential components. The first step is to silence the critical voice that you hear in your head. The second step is to initiate a regimen of self-compassionate practices.

According to findings from studies on self-esteem, individuals might experience emotional and social difficulties regardless of whether they have a high or low sense of their own value. While high levels of self-esteem have been connected to narcissism and aggressive behaviors, low levels of self-esteem have been linked to social anxiety, passiveness, and depression. The kind of self-esteem that is best for one's mental health is a moderate form of self-esteem that is based on recognizing one's inherent worth as a person rather than comparing oneself to the worth of other people. In this sense, if your goal is to create more self-confidence, it is better to focus on having high levels of self-worth rather than high levels of self-esteem. This is because self-worth is a measure of how much you value yourself.

In therapy, one's sense of self-worth is frequently discussed. Acceptance and comprehension are two qualities that can help a person feel better about themselves. You may assist yourself by keeping an eye on the conversations that are going on in your head, giving yourself credit for your achievements, practicing tolerance and assertiveness, and hanging out with your friends. Improving one's sense of self-worth can be accomplished through recognizing and appreciating one's own abilities and strengths, acknowledging and honoring one's own intelligence, and taking one's own emotions and worldviews into account. To maintain a healthy equilibrium, it is necessary to be able to direct your attention toward other people.

At The Office, Body Language

Being able to converse and write well are only two aspects of having excellent relational talents; there is also something else involved. It is possible that you will need to focus on your body language of agreement in order to be a good communicator in your place of employment. Being alert, sympathetic, and observant are all essential components of accurate body language interpretation. In the following paragraphs, we will define body language, discuss how it is typically deployed, and provide a few examples of the impact it may have in the workplace.

WHAT EXACTLY IS BODY LANGUAGE, ANYWAY?

The word "body language" refers to all the non-verbal communication tactics that people use. Messages that are transmitted between people without the use of words are known as non-verbals. The term "body language" refers to outward looks, movements, attitudes, and other indicators that are developmentally based. In order to communicate clearly and effectively, it is common practice to combine verbal messages with body language. The use of appropriate body language is one of the most crucial aspects of any correspondence nearly all of the time. The following are examples of specific types of body language:

The outward manifestations of one's emotions, such as smirking, staring, or acting out an exasperated expression

Signals made with the hands, such as waving, beckoning someone to get closer, or relying on the tips of your fingers

Constant adopting of postures such as slouching, sitting up straight, or leaning forward by someone

Several distinct types of gestures, such as giving someone the middle finger, clapping, or shaking their hand.

AT THE OFFICE, BODY LANGUAGE

In the workplace, one's body language can communicate a wide range of ideas and emotions. The use of body language is prevalent in both private and public forms of communication. You are likely to employ some type of body language if you have a conversation with a coworker, take part in a meeting, or meet a customer. These activities all fall under the category of "meetings."

Throughout the course of a workday, one's body language may send several important messages. In a significant way, a person's level of interest or their fundamental interest can be deduced from their body language. If someone makes eye contact with you, gestures at you while you talk, or leans toward you while you are talking, it is likely that they are giving you their whole consideration. It's possible that someone is exhausted or distracted if they're shifting in their seat, turning their back on you repeatedly, or fidgeting with their fingers. It is helpful to be able to recognize and interpret these messages if you need to determine how an individual or a group reacts to the ideas or suggestions that you have presented.

Learning how to read and use body language in the workplace can have a significant impact on the overall profitability and connections of the group. You will significantly improve your skills as a professional communicator if you are able to accurately interpret body language. While you are working to improve your perception of body language in the workplace, it is essential for you to think about several key realities pertaining to body language.

To begin, the surrounding environment is an essential component in the process of interpreting body language. There are some occupations that, depending on the person doing them and the circumstances, might have an entirely different meaning. An expression of dissatisfaction or sorrow can be conveyed through the use of crossed arms. Regardless of this, for certain people, they can also convey a sense of assurance or a carefree demeanor. If you are comfortable with your superiors, coworkers, or clients, you will be able to read their exceptional body language far more successfully.

You will be able to comprehend messages that are not spoken aloud for everyone to hear if you have a good grasp of body language at the workplace. This is one of the advantages of having a good understanding of body language. The words that someone speaks can either be supported or refuted by the non-verbal messages they send. A coworker might subtly nod their head while saying, "I totally concur with what you're saying," which is an indication of agreement. A customer might say, "I am really not intrigued," while leaning forward in their seat and expressing this sentiment. These muddled communications may be meaningless at times, but they also have the potential to give you some insightful information about what another person is thinking.

1.2 A very brief introduction to Westernization and the process of globalization

You might be asking why I wish to explore this topic here; nevertheless, the purpose of this book is to assist you in better comprehending the media-driven culture in which we currently exist. It worries me that you might bypass any of these chapters, but I can't stress enough how vital it is that you don't do that.

Understanding this aspect of media theory is beneficial when considering the media in its entirety, despite the fact that you probably won't be attempting to accomplish #SciComm on a global scale most of the time. There is also the possibility that your audience in the digital domains will be people from all over the world.

It's better to establish a large audience than have one suddenly arise then slowly fade away as people lose interest because then the global media globe becomes important to what you have to say than to have the misfortune of going viral and having the digital equivalent of 15 minutes of fame. Despite this, it's possible that the term "nine days' wonder," which dates back to Elizabethan times, is more fitting given how much longer digital lasts.

The purpose of this section is to provide you with an understanding of a significant component of media theory from a perspective that is distinct from one that you may already be considering. Globalization is seen as a negative phenomenon by the vast majority of people, despite the fact that it has contributed to improvements in living conditions and educational opportunities across the globe. When viewed in this light, science is a global endeavor, and it is true that it does alter the course of history.

You have probably been exposed to the concept of the Global Village, which holds a pretty significant place in the realm of media. Marshall McLuhan is the person who is most closely linked with it, and the fundamental concept behind it is that as the 20th century proceeded, we all started to become more connected, see the same things in the media, and started to become more alike.

There is a connection to Westernization as a result of the fact that those of us living in the West, notably the United States of America and Hollywood, are exerting a greater influence on the global media landscape than any other nation or region. You might be asking what relevance this has to the field of scientific communication, but please stay with me; we are not competing in a race at this point. There is nothing new about globalization; in fact, you could argue that the history of the past 2,000 years is the history of globalization. Globalization has been going on for a very long time. The ancient Greeks and Romans practiced it, as did the major nations of Europe at the time, and of course, religion appears to have a strong interest in the practice.

At this point in time, globalization in its modern sense is accomplished mostly through the medium of the media as well as the ongoing process of westernization. Since this isn't a lesson in history, I won't spend too much time going over the past. However, it is essential that you realize that this is just one part of a long, continuous wave of how humans connect with one another and strive to spread their ideas and ideals to the rest of the globe.

It used to be done with a sword, but now days it's done with the media.

Watching a movie is all that is required in order to illustrate how this process of globalization works. Hollywood is one of the most important media producers in the world since its products are shown pretty much everywhere and are exported to other countries. There was a time when the government of the United States even established a department dedicated to helping make this a reality.

When we watch television, we most likely watch American sitcoms or dramas. This is not to say that we just watch these types of shows, but we do watch them. Even while we watch the news, events are unfolding; CNN has a significant influence on how we perceive it, and the majority of news programs throughout the world now have the same format. The global news media is aired all around the world, even on our very own national broadcasters here in the United States.

And then there's the internet, which goes without saying. Not only do we have access to all of the information in the globe, but we also have the power to communicate with every single person on the planet.

If I understand it correctly, globalization results in our becoming more similar to one another.

No, not quite like that.

While China restricts the number of Hollywood films that can be released in the country, France and India both have their own film companies that are quite successful. The pictures and messages conveyed in a film cannot be altered, despite the fact that the language used in the film can be modified. Films are said to be "set in stone." However, the fact that the message is being transmitted does not guarantee that it will also be the message that is received. Perhaps, just possibly, someone, somewhere, supports Darth Vader because they believe that maintaining law and order is more essential than preserving individual liberties. Hashtag: #NotMyEmperor

It is possible to modify the news media; all you need to do is look at how Fox News has politicized television news in the United States and newspapers in the United Kingdom to understand how the same story can be transformed to provide different meanings to audiences in each country.

We can look at Globalization as the driving force behind Westernization; yet, if the news can be adjusted to match the expectations of the audience, and how the viewer perceives the media reflects how they comprehend it, then clearly this does not assist you get your message through effectively.

And what are your thoughts on the Internet's potential to serve as a positive force in the process of globalization? Every one of us has access to the same information, can read the same articles, and can communicate with one another. However, do we?

In our own lives, without even realizing it, we limit ourselves to Dunbar's Number, which is a hypothesis that says the maximum number of individuals with whom we can maintain meaningful relationships is between 120 and 150. Or, to put it another way, evolution causes us to have a strong desire to be with our own kind.

It is something that happens to all of us, whether it is that we accept new members or allow some to leave the group. You can see this in your digital life, as the average number of friends a person has on Facebook is 120, and you'll know from here that we share friends with strangers, and so our tribes can get bigger or smaller, cross pollination with other tribes like a digital Venn diagram. This is something that you can see in your own digital life.

Now we can see that the Internet is actually performing the exact opposite of what we believe it to be doing. In his book "The Myth of Media Globalization," Kai Hafez addresses this topic. The early Internet, which was an invention of the western world, was only available in the English language. However, it is now common knowledge that countries have the web available in their own language, and the news media is repackaged online for each part of the world.

I used to have a job where I could see a video of a fishing boat going down in real time, and it was fascinating. After uploading the video to the social media accounts, I waited for it to be picked up by both national and local news organizations before it started to go viral all over the world.

I was able to witness how the news reports changed through a succession of Chinese Whispers and Broken Telephone processes as they traveled from one region to the next over the course of a period of four hours. The news article was the same, but different countries reported it differently.

The question now is, what factors are responsible for these divergent accounts? To put it plainly, the culture.

We have a tendency in the western world to believe that we have all become the same, and if you have this belief, I encourage you to travel to France and ask the people there if it is true. The values held in France are distinct from those held in North America. And in the region of North America, Canada, the United States of America, and Mexico all have quite distinct cultural norms and beliefs.

Because of my own experience working in communications in the UK, I can tell you that the culture varies from one region to another and needs to be taken into consideration regardless of whether you are concentrating on local or national communications. And this doesn't even take into account the myriad of distinct subcultures that exist throughout diverse sectors of society.

Therefore, the "global village" is not so much a village as it is a notion of communities that are connected to each other and talk to each other in a variety of different ways. On top of that lies the westernization that occurs through the media. This westernization is received, but it is not necessarily perceived the way it was intended to be, or even completely modified to satisfy the requirements of the local community. Teenagers in Japan are a great illustration of this principle being put into practice.

THE DEVELOPMENT OF TIMING PROGRAMS

Paper, individual sheets of paper, and colored pencils are required supplies for this activity.

The bare minimum required is between 20 and 25 persons.

Time: around a quarter of an hour

The development of norms and routines is extremely important for children and adolescents who have AS. As a result, these individuals maintain a record of what is going to take place, which lowers their levels of tension and anxiety.

Putting individuals into relevant groups. Everyone has been given the instruction to write down the responsibilities they fulfill on a daily basis and arrange them in descending order of importance.

After the first part has been broken down and completed, the next step is to examine the significance of organizing the responsibilities that are carried out on a daily basis in order to take into account the successful completion of each and every one of them without missing any of them.

The participants are provided with orientations to develop schedules, and they have the ability to create these schedules in tables, putting them in the order of significance, and timing each event. It is possible for them to be accompanied by drawings or photos that serve to beautify them and make them more appealing.

There will be time at the end of the activity for participants to discuss how they felt and to explain how the activity developed. This will provide structure and order to the activities that have been carried out.

Children and adolescents who have AS benefit from playing this game because it helps them better control the feelings brought on by the timely fulfillment of each commitment, which in turn lessens the anxiety they experience in anticipation of events that have not yet taken place.

Both Confidence And Communication Are Essential For Success.

Communication is what you should aim for whenever you have a conversation with another person, regardless of whether they are complete strangers or somebody you have known for a long time. To hear and to be heard at the same time. You want to not only make a good impression on people, but also form friendships that will last a long time. It goes without saying that the relevance of confidence and good communication etiquette in these settings must not be underestimated. Whether you're on a stage delivering a speech or you're chatting to individuals, the importance of these traits cannot be overstated. You can tell how well you know yourself and how confident you are in your own talents by the way you carry yourself and how confident you appear to others. It's possible that at initially, some people will find the initial shyness and lack of directness to be endearing, but over time, this will likely change. The dangers do not disappear after this point. Ineffective communication skills, such as hurriedly making your point of view or completely neglecting your speaking partner, are just two examples of the kinds of behaviors that can stymie the flow of a productive conversation. Even if we may despise the tight knot that forms in our throats when we stand in front of a new person to speak or the feeling of being misunderstood by those we hold in high regard, it is possible that we will have to deal with situations like these at every significant crossroads in our lives. It might quite literally make the difference between ascending up the ladder of success and tragically tumbling down the ladder of failure. But how can we build up enough self-assurance to feel comfortable speaking in public? First and foremost, there needs to be faith in oneself. You have, without a doubt, been exposed to similar material in the past. To put it simply, it cannot be denied. Your voice will serve as the vehicle for transporting the message to be conveyed. The same way that you can't fly to a distant nation or sail across the seas if you don't have an aircraft or a boat, the same way that your words can't get from your lips to the ears of your listeners if you don't use your voice. In the same way that a pilot has to have faith in both the plane he is flying and in his own ability to do so in a competent and secure manner, you have to have faith that your voice will deliver your words in an unharmed manner. It's not shyness, but rather self-doubt that can ruin a decent conversation most of the time. You start to question whether or not you are using the necessary words, whether or not your voice is irritating or nice enough, whether or not you are dressed appropriately, and whether or not the person or persons you are speaking with are even paying attention. You let your thoughts become consumed by all of these concerns, and as a result, you lose track of who you are. Before you open your mouth, you should be sure to check in with yourself and determine the feelings that are racing through your mind. Regain your composure. Adopting these recommendations will provide you with the poise and self-assurance you need to communicate clearly and effectively:

A common misunderstanding is that this one specific component is responsible for the dissolution of innumerable marriages and other types of familial connections. Unfortuitously, it is possible for two or more people to get into a fight even when they are essentially saying the same things and further making the same arguments. This can happen even though they are expressing the same things. The majority of the time, this occurs when whoever is speaking not only tries to persuade the other person but also wants to demonstrate the other person's lack of intelligence. They succeed in doing this, but in the process, they misunderstand something that was said, lose sight of the flow of the conversation, and stop listening to the person who is speaking. When they do finally tune back into the conversation, they mistake something that was said. It's possible that they misunderstood, but they feel a flush of pride in their decision to ask for clarification. They come to the wrong conclusions, which leads to the formation of rifts.

Be Direct: A lot of the time, when we say things, we are not direct in the way that we speak. When we are trying to emphasize our arguments, we could decide to provide an excessive amount of story. It's possible that we do this in an effort to better explain ourselves to others, or maybe just to make sure that they don't get the wrong impression of us. There is also the possibility that we will give analogies, make the topic esoteric, etc. Whoever is listening will eventually become disoriented as a result of this, and they will lose interest in whatever is being said. This is frequently brought on by a lack of self-confidence or the worry that one will be turned down. You should avoid being rude, but it's okay to be straightforward while you're talking to make things easier and more pleasurable for everyone involved.

Take heed:

When we talk to other people, we want them to feel that their ideas and perspectives are being taken into consideration and that their thoughts are being heard. to the point where it requires our attention. When having a discussion with another person, you should avoid being so preoccupied with your own ideas or the things you are doing at the time that you fail to pay attention to the other person. You are free to interrupt them at any moment during the chat and offer questions that will help you better understand the point that is being conveyed. This not only shows that you are present in the moment but also enhances the confidence of the person who is speaking, encouraging them to engage in more open and honest conversation with you.

Why Do We Waste Our Time With Inane Chitchat?

Small chat is a skill that a lot of people consider to be pointless to possess since they believe it takes up too much time. Small chat is beneficial as a helpful bonding ritual, and it also contributes to maintaining proper inter-personal distance by striking a balance between being too nosy and being too detached.

There are many benefits to making and maintaining casual conversation. First, as was noted earlier, making light conversation might lead to previously closed doors being opened. The nature of the relationship that exists between coworkers, acquaintances, and friends can be better understood through idle small talk or chatter. A simple activity like this one enables new acquaintances to learn more about each other's roles in society and to classify this information in accordance with their deductions.

The primary idea that underpins the practice of small talk is the unwavering requirement placed on an individual to maintain a cheerful demeanor at all times. This is done in an effort to elicit favorable responses from others who are in close proximity to the individual, including friends, coworkers, acquaintances, and strangers alike.

In a social engagement, small talk acts as a lubricant, helping to smooth out awkward gaps or periods of silence that are bound to occur owing to the nature of interactions in general. The purpose of small talk shifts depending on the stage of the discussion at which it is employed.

The beginning of a conversation

When two individuals are meeting one another for the first time, small chat is a means for them to show that they want to get along with one another and be nice. Conversations about insignificant topics can help set the stage for a future relationship.

People may form snap judgments about one other's levels of knowledge, experience, reputation, and intentions during the very first interaction that they have with one another during a business meeting.

When the two persons interacting have had a previous relationship or have had a casual interaction, small chat acts as a gentle introduction to refresh the memory and serves as a precursor for a more functional conversation. Small talk can also be used when the two people interacting are meeting for the first time.

That wraps up our talk.

There are times when you suddenly find that you have run out of topics to talk about, which can lead to an unpleasant lull in the conversation. This abrupt breakup can frequently leave the other person with the impression that they have been rejected. Small chat can assist prevent a scenario like this from occurring by easing the transition between two individuals, easing the pain of rejection, and turning it into an affirmation in an uncomplicated manner.

In order to fill the voids

Silences are typically awkward because people tend to keep their eyes darting about or gaze at each other in an uncomfortable manner, which can result in a situation that is awkward for both parties. Humans are social animals, and despite the passage of time, the animal impulses that are still a part of us have not been completely extinguished. Because in the animal kingdom, silence is equated to a sign that there is a potential danger about, this is why periods of stillness sound silent warning bells in our heads: because in the animal world, silence is equal to a message that there is a potential danger around.

Small conversation is helpful for reducing stress and filling the silence with mindless banter while waiting for a more useful topic to come up.

In many of the interactions that people have, the small talk has no real purpose at all. It's nothing more than a casual chat with someone you just know on a surface level. For instance:

Matt: How are you tonight, Lily?

Lily: How are you tonight, Matt? How have you been?

Matt: No, I'm OK. Where do you stand?

Lily: You sound fine to me. How was your weekend, generally speaking?

Matt: Yes, you are correct. Did you do it?

Yes, I am Lily, and I am grateful that you asked. Will get back to you later on.

Ok, see you later, Matt.

This is a textbook illustration of how the entire conversation consisted of little more than idle chitchat. We have a propensity to conduct these kinds of interactions with people we only tangentially know, such as when we unexpectedly meet into a coworker in a setting other than the office or when we run into someone we met briefly at a party.

The entirety of the talk is meaningless nonsense that serves no purpose and is only there to fill space.

The relationship between two individuals and the level of mutual comprehension can be gauged by the amount of small chat they engage in with one another. An indicator of the level of intimacy that exists between a couple is the fact that they avoid engaging in meaningless small talk. There is no such thing as "awkward silences" in their chats, and even if the conversation runs out, they can be comfortable while it is silent. This is in contrast to casual friends, who would feel awkward if they were put in a position similar to this one.

Small conversation is something that frequently occurs between coworkers who are in the same position. Managers frequently engage in idle chitchat with the employees who report to them in order to facilitate the development of relationships with those employees and to establish positive rapport with those employees in order to improve the quality of the working environment.

It's possible for managers and owners to push their employees to work harder and longer by engaging in idle chatter with them. The employees are given the impression that their employer is on the same level as them and one of them as a result of the small conversation that managers and owners participate in, rather than viewing their boss as an authoritative figure who compels them to work against their will.

Small talk and functional conversations are two distinct types of discussions that can take place in the workplace. The distinction between the two depends on the persons having the conversation as well as their relationships with one another and the organizational structure. When a superior and one of his subordinates are having a conversation, it is typically the superior who "takes charge" of the conversation, meaning that he or she is the one who sets the tone for the conversation and determines who is "in charge." This is due to the fact that, as a result of his dominance, he is able to skip over the idle chatter and get immediately to a subject that is more useful and important.

These are only some of the reasons why we participate in meaningless conversation and small talk with our contemporaries as well as complete strangers.

EVALUATING ONE'S PARTICIPATION IN THE LOCAL COMMUNITY

People that suffer from autism spectrum disorders struggle when it comes to generalization. This indicates that they do not have the ability to transfer information, knowledge, or habits from one environment to another. For instance, a person's experience of going through the lunch line at school is not likely to adequately prepare them for the experience of ordering lunch at a fast food restaurant.

Because of this, it's possible that the evaluation of community events will need to be very individualized and very location- and activity-specific. You can't assume that a different environment won't require some particular considerations simply because the student can effectively participate in the routines in one setting; just because they can do so in one setting doesn't mean they always will.

Training opportunities are being expanded into community settings through an increasing number of educational programs. Instead of making assumptions about how the student would handle interactions and transactions in the community, it will be more informative to see how the student handles them. In addition to producing greater results, training that takes place in a communal setting is superior than simulations of the events.

The structure of your evaluation should be comprised of four primary questions, despite the fact that observations will provide a wealth of information.

1. Does the student appear to be making progress with their current performance? Does the learner successfully do what he is seeking to complete in a clear and purposeful manner without experiencing unusually high levels of difficulty? Does his behavior indicate that he understands

the demands that the environment places on him?

2. Is the performance as it is currently effective? Are you able to complete the activities quickly and simply with a minimum of confusion or frustration?

3. Are the strategies currently in place for achieving student goals simple to implement? Is the information that everyone engaged needs to comprehend readily available to them?

4. Does the current system accurately reflect the requirements of the community? Does it encourage the community to participate and make it easy for them to do so? Does it take into account the time limits that are typically present in public settings?

5. Is the training designed to help participants become more self-sufficient in their performance of the goals?

Your observations will be guided as you identify specific community activities to evaluate by the assessment titled COMMUNICATION IN THE COMMUNITY. You will assess the environment, identify specific communication skills necessary to successfully participate in that environment, and evaluate the student's performance in that activity. The responses to these questions will build a framework from which you may make decisions on (1) what skills to teach, (2) what environmental supports are already available for the student to use, and (3) where visual tools might provide further help to raise the student's level of independence.

How to Be Confident in Your Own Voice

The degree to which one is assertive has a significant bearing on communication overall. When you have the appropriate body language and when you select the right words to speak, you will find that your communication is more expressive, more clear, and also more forceful. When you have the right body language and when you choose the right words to speak. There are a few strategies and pointers that you can follow in order to acquire that level of assertiveness:

Rather than only making a statement, I will state.

There are times when you may utter words without fully comprehending the effect that those words will have on the people to whom they are directed. In situations like these, you are breaching the first and most essential rule of assertiveness, which is to respect the rights of other people. The most harmful of all of these types of sentences are the ones that directly address the reader with the word "you." Instead of focusing on what another person did, you should emphasize how you feel about the situation. This can be accomplished through the use of "I" expressions such as "when you do not deliver on time, I feel angry."

Having an attitude that is not one of judgment

At a very young age, we are conditioned to believe that it is important to categorize other individuals and give them names. Our ego instructs us to behave in a judgmental manner so that we can maintain a sense of separation from other people and achieve this goal. In the course of the procedure, effective communication will be lost. People who are quick to pass judgment are prone to making statements like "he or she is stupid." An assertive person, on the other hand, is one who makes an attempt to evaluate a situation and comprehend the reasons why another person makes certain errors.

To Be More Specific

It is not a sign of boldness to make assertions that are not particular but rather make generalizations about anything. When someone is forceful, the remarks that they make are ones that are true to the facts. It is essential to provide factual information. The goal of ensuring that clear communication is achieved will not be served by generalization.

Arguments Against Being an Assertive Person

There are some women who make the choice to not speak up for themselves. Fear is the typical motivating factor behind this decision. Sometimes it's because they question the value of what they have to offer. There is no valid excuse for someone to not be forceful, regardless of the justification that they give.

In the following paragraphs, I will discuss some of the most widespread reasons why women choose not to speak their minds.

People are going to become upset with me.

This is wholly motivated by apprehension of possible retribution or rejection. The line of thought goes something like this: "If I am assertive, X will get mad at me because I am making it difficult for them to do things their way." When people lose their cool, negative events almost always follow. Therefore, let's not make folks angry, shall we?

If you put off satisfying your wants and needs out of concern for the responses of other people, you could experience less discomfort in the short term; nevertheless, in the long run, this behavior will lead to dissatisfaction, wrath, and resentment.

People are going to feel harmed.

This mode of thinking is propelled forward by an overwhelming sense of guilt. It originates from the idea that if one person gets their way, it means that someone else won't get theirs. I've made several references throughout this book to the idea that genuine assertiveness is making every effort to find a resolution that benefits both parties. Even if that isn't possible, there is no reason for you to fear that someone will feel awful or break apart as a result of your having expressed your opinion and having things work out in a way that is beneficial to you.

If you assert yourself in a courteous manner, you shouldn't let it keep you up at night. When someone is assertive, they are not conspiring with others in order to get what they want; there is no underhandedness involved. Being assertive means communicating in an open and honest manner while also allowing events to follow their natural course.

I don't think people will like me.

When it finally dawned on me that not everyone I meet will take a liking to me, it was an unpleasant revelation to say the least. In many situations, I won't even need to do or say anything since they won't like how I style my hair, how I apply my cosmetics, the clothes I wear, or any of the other things I do. However, do you know what? That's not a problem! Even I don't get along with everyone I come in contact with. It's a human being. When you are aware of this, it is much simpler to overcome the concern that when you assert yourself, others will stop like you. It is not a form of nagging to express your viewpoint. Putting in a request for anything is not annoying. It is not your concern if other people have that kind of experience with it. Keep in mind what you just read: it has nothing to do with you what other people think about you.

If you know how to be forceful in the appropriate way, no one will find it reason to despise you. I can nearly guarantee that. When you act aggressively or passive-aggressively, that is the moment when they will be the least impressed by you. A little bit later on, you are going to get an explanation of all of the differences.

If you can't say anything good, don't say anything at all...

When I didn't have anything constructive to say, my mother instilled in me the importance of maintaining my composure and remaining silent. It's likely that someone told you the same thing or something very similar. When it comes to assertiveness, this advice is completely irrelevant and should not be followed. Why? Because being assertive does not mean being rude or disrespectful; rather, it is something that goes hand in hand with having respect.

When you are assertive, you don't let things build up until you explode, which reduces the possibility that you will say something that you will later come to regret. Instead, you remain level-headed and composed in the face of challenges, waiting for them to present themselves before responding appropriately.

It is not a major issue.

Before I learnt to be more forceful, I would say things like this on a daily basis. I've since changed my ways. I can still recall the sensation I'd have on the inside at the time. Fear, shame, and a healthy dose of self-deprecation were all present in that moment. I didn't consider myself important enough to be able to say "No, I don't agree," therefore I was willing to comply with whatever was proposed. It's hardly a huge deal, is it? Not true!

It is not a healthy approach to life to minimize your own wants and needs and to disregard your boundaries in order to meet the wants and needs of others. It will only serve to reinforce the notion that you are beneath others, and it will have no positive effect on the self-esteem you now possess.

You need to learn to catch yourself before you say anything that will push your wants, ideals, or opinions to the background. You have every right to fight for the things that are important to you.

People are already aware of my intentions.

It would be wonderful if everyone have psychic abilities, but the reality is that this is probably not the case. You can't expect other people to guess what you want or how you're feeling just based on what you say. If you believe that other people are aware of what is going on inside of your head, you are setting yourself up for disappointment. Assuming that another person should intuitively understand how to fulfill your needs and fulfill your happiness comes across as highly selfish.

Tell them what you want rather than keeping quiet and hope that someone will figure it out on their own. When you are sharing your expectations with them, be as direct as possible. If there is no room for misunderstanding and everybody is on the same page, then the likelihood of you getting what you want will be significantly increased.

That wraps up some of the more broad considerations that go into why women might choose not to be forceful. Nevertheless, I believe it is necessary to investigate the reasons why working women are less likely to express their opinions, argue with others, bargain, or advocate for themselves. Examine the next section to see if any of the points connect to you in any way.

Everything a Project Manager Needs to Know Concerning the Management of Conflict

A strong skill set is required of a project manager. And one of the most challenging aspects to comprehend is how to deal with dispute. It's not something you'll use every day, I hope. However, you will require it on occasion in the future. It doesn't matter if you're asked to settle a minor disagreement or diffuse a major disagreement; conflict management should be an essential part of your toolset for managing projects.

There will inevitably be conflict.

Conflict is inevitable; it doesn't matter how skillfully you manage projects or how adept you are at dealing with people. It just does. When individuals care about something that is new, important, and complex, it is natural that they will do so. In addition, there are instances when it is beneficial to vigorously debate contrasting points of view.

A Tutorial on How to Handle Conflict

The first part of our two-part guide to managing conflict is presented here in this chapter. The second section will be covered in the following chapter. In this article, we will cover all the basics for you about conflict management, including the following:

The First Section: Laying the Groundwork

What really is the conflict?

Recognizing the Warning Signs of a Worsening Conflict

The Core Ideas Behind Effective Conflict Management

The following are five methods for resolving conflict:

Components for the Resolution of Disputes Between Members of the Team

Steps to Take in the Real World, Part 2

The Process of Managing Conflict in Steps

Advice on How to Handle Conflicts

Positive Attitudes to Foster Effective Conflict Management

Reestablishing Connections After They Have Been Broken

However, there is no point in dithering around, so let's just get right down to business!

What really is the conflict?

Projects are what bring about change. And opposition to change is inevitable.

Everywhere you discover resistance, there is a chance that it will eventually turn into confrontation.

Ambrose Bierce is credited with having said, "Speak when you are angry, and you will make the best speech you will ever regret."

The fact that we hold diverse beliefs and priorities about what should be emphasized almost guarantees that we will have disagreements. As a result, we engage in conflict either to defend the values and views that are important to us or to try to convince others that we are in the right.

If you end up in a situation where you need to resolve a problem, seek for ways to do so behind closed doors. Because when you are in front of an audience, you will have the feeling that you need to 'perform' for them, and you will also have less opportunity to listen, hear, or reevaluate your stance. Your only strategy will be to vigorously defend your pitch.

Know How to Say It When You Need to Say Something is the Topic of Chapter 7.

It would be wonderful if I could say that you can totally avoid finding yourself in a scenario where you're having a conversation with many people at the same time, but there is no assurance that you will absolutely never find yourself in this kind of setting. It would be nice if I could say that you can completely avoid finding yourself in a situation where you're having a conversation with many people at the same time. When you find yourself in a scenario where you have to communicate verbally with a group of people, this chapter is going to offer you some suggestions on how you can behave verbally. Wouldn't it be good if, instead of putting your head down to avoid interacting with others or being silent during the entirety of the conversation, you were self-assured and well-prepared? This chapter is going to focus entirely on that topic, so be sure to come prepared. After reading this chapter, you will have a better grasp of strategies that you may employ while you are in a conversation that will offer your personality with an outward portrayal of risk, engagement, and confidence, even if you do not internally feel as though you possess these traits. This is because these strategies will allow you to provide your personality with an outward portrayal of risk, engagement, and confidence.

The Influence of Being Interrupted

For someone who does not necessarily enjoy talking in crowds of people, interrupting may be one of the only ways that they are going to be able to get a word into the conversation. Sure, you've probably been told that interrupting is rude ever since you were a little kid, and there are certainly times when this is true. However, for someone who does not necessarily enjoy talking in crowds of people, this may be one of the only ways that they are going to be able to get a word into the conversation. This is especially the case if individuals are not accustomed to hearing much from you. It is vital to refrain from interrupting a conversation unless you have something to add or a question that is directly related to the topic at hand. When you have decided to interrupt, further helpful advice is to make sure that your voice is loud, strong, and unwavering in pitch. This is especially important if you are trying to get someone's attention. If you don't stop talking, the person you've interrupted can continue talking as if you hadn't said anything at all. If something like this does occur, resist the urge to become disheartened.

If you're afraid to try out this strategy, you should first make an effort to track the instances in which others interrupt you when you're speaking with other people. This will give you a better idea of how to respond to interruptions in the future. It takes much more frequently than you might imagine, and as a result, there is really no justification for you not to take part in it as well. Who knows, you could even find that you enjoy cutting other people off in conversation at some point in your life. If you do have this feeling, make sure you don't let it get the better of you and preserve your composure.

Maintain Your Strength After Your Activity Has Been Interrupted

If you're an introvert, another helpful strategy to put into practice is to pay attention to the times when other people cut you off in conversation. If you are someone who keeps to themselves during a discussion, you might be startled to discover, once you start paying attention to it, how frequently others cut you off in the middle of what you are saying. Extroverts, as opposed to introverts, enjoy engaging in conversation. They are the undisputed kings of verbal diarrhea. This means that even if you are only pausing for a second to take a breath of air during a discussion, an extroverted person may start to take control of the conversation and continue talking while you are thinking about what you want to say next. When someone interrupts you, even if you don't feel like it's a big deal to you personally, it sends the message that what you have to say is less important than what the other person is attempting to cram into the conversation. Because of this, it is essential that you protect your space inside the dialogue; this is due to the fact that your ideas and emotions are of the utmost significance.

If someone does interrupt you and you're ready to put an end to this kind of scenario, the simplest step you can take to prevent it from happening again is to simply confront the person who interrupted you head-on. You could say something like, "Can I just finish my thought before you begin yours?" or "I gave you your turn, now let me have mine." Other possible phrases include: "I will let you have your turn now." When you make statements of this nature to a person with whom you are having a conversation, it is of the utmost importance that you do it with a friendly smile on your face and a spring in your step when you speak. If you disregard the significance of the language that your body conveys, you run the risk of coming across as upset or offended. You will be in a much stronger position to maintain your position if you can come up with a way to bring some humor into the scenario while you are doing your best to maintain it.

www.ingramcontent.com/pod-product-compliance
Lightning Source LLC
Chambersburg PA
CBHW050234120526
44590CB00016B/2088